Poetic Seeds

Cultivating Thoughts & Ideas

By: Annie Laura Degrafinreid

Poetic Seeds

Cultivating

Thoughts & Ideas

Poems By:

Annie Laura Degrafinreid

Illustrator: Digitalhandart

ISBN: 9780578891460

Library of Congress Control Number: 2021909684

Any references to historical events real people or real places are used fictitiously names, characters, and places are products of the author's imagination. Printed by Kindle Direct Publishing, Inc., In the United States of America.

Kindle Direct Publishing (KDP`).

Seattle Washington

Acknowledgement

I thank God for
Bringing all of my thoughts into captivity,
And for turning them into poetic expressions.

Special thanks to my daughter Sakeenah
For encouraging me to publish my poems
And for assuring me that now is the time.
Sakeenah, thank you for reading, re-reading, editing
And providing invaluable technical support and advice.

To my dear friend June,
Your unwavering support and knowledge base
Over the years
Has always colored my endeavors.
Much appreciation!!

And to Shanus, my #1 son
THANK YOU for listening to and critiquing
Those hot off the press selections,
Your opinion mattered!!

To my trusted friend Debbie
Who boosted my literary prowess
After reading my 1st set of poems
Many thanks!!

Dedication

To my late sister Ada Boyd who has always made me
Believe that I could do anything…
I miss you and I love you!!

About the Author

Annie Laura Degrafinreid was born in Tennessee but has
Lived most of her adult life in Long Island, New York.
For as long as I can remember, she has been a creative
Wordsmith. Annie has written plays, skits, short stories
And of course prose and poetry. On many levels, This
poetess has been scattering seeds of hope and
Encouragement for decades. She is an Adelphi University
Graduate with an extensive professional history in
Mental Health Services. Annie
is a retired social worker With
decades of experience.
She has given up clinical charting to creatively capture
The pulse of the human spirit through the art of poetry.
Writing new and original lines with a poetic flow has
Become her passion.
On the path to relaxation, Annie is totally enjoying
Her two grandchildren, Aminah and Andrew. She
loves gardening, the theatre
And has recently found a new love for the culinary arts.
However, nothing is more relaxing to her than
Watching the sun rise and glisten Over
the ocean on early morning walks.

By: Sakeenah N. Williams

Contents

Introduction

Portions of Poetic Seeds germinated on the shelf In
and out of darkness for decades. Other seeds Seeking
light patiently waited for the zenith hour. Then there
were those very special poems blessed by Insight,
inspired by love or just life itself that enjoyed The
flow. Breathing oxygen, expressions grew like
Wildflowers manifesting themselves into varying styles
And genres. Each verse found roots In reality
And grounded itself into a therapeutic base.
Overall, these verses became a product of humanity With
insight and hope for a harmonious future. Whether
concrete or fleeting, real or imaginary
Abstract or analytical, they have all culminated into this
Complete book of poetry titled Poetic Seeds.

The life infusion of this body of work has been
Transformed into eleven segments. Self-reflective,
These organized selections are presented as seeds.
By design, and for your reading pleasure
Each seed is age and gender friendly.
In this garden of lyrics and rhymes
Some poems are inspired by true life events
Or stories as observed by the author.
It is my hope that this little book of poetry will
Find a home in your library,
Book collection or kindle read.
I encourage you to pursue your passion
And explore the power of your voice.

Chapter 1

Cultivating Seeds Has Just Begun Find Motivation In Chapter One

<u>*Seeds of Motivation*</u>

Reflection

I'm not me anymore as you can see
I'm a speck a morsel a reflection of me.

I'm all that I've seen and everywhere I've been I'm
colossal, miniscule and somewhere in between. I'm
a child at heart trapped in an adult's body Insecure
silly at times a little naughty.

Stepping out… tip-toeing across my comfort zone
Experiencing having a mind of my own.
Still discovering my options and owning my choices
Learning that consequences are always unavoidable.

I'm not me anymore as you can see
I'm a grand total of all that I can be.

I'm a bunch of emotions clustered in the heart
A stumble a struggle a complete overhaul.
I'm the spark that once shimmered bright in both eyes,
One salty teardrop an internal cry.

But as you can see…
I'm not me
I'm one BIG quest for all that I can be!!

Metamorphosis

A fierce North wind that ceases to blow
A lone star flickers before losing its glow
Daffodils and Morning glories
Disappear in the Fall.

As change goes Seasons know
In almost total recall
When one life ends another begins
Be it Winter, Summer, Spring or Fall.

As the cycle of both life and death
Begins with a change
We are once again reminded
That nothing stays the same.

Challenges strengthen character
As the mountain will not move Natural
disasters transcend expectations
Reaching another level of endurance.
With each change comes assurance.

So as Daffodils and Morning glories
Disappear in the Fall
They seek comfort in their resting state
With total recall.

Impulsivity

Flashing yellow lights, no caution allowed
I live in the moment impulse is my guide.
Make my decisions quick
On raw emotions
No thought or plan given to my notions.
I act without thinking
Make my own way
Ponder not on decisions from day to day.

One blurt… a word… then
A quick reaction
Has been my recipe for pure disaster. Then
I can't retract or fix the damage done
So I readjust and live on the run.
In reality…
It's difficult to admit
That my true survival is illicit.

I dream of wondering and thinking twice
Have nightmares about analyzing and
Taking advice.
But I continue on in my green light zone
Often feeling isolated and alone.
Knowing deep in my soul I must admit
That acting on impulse has been my detriment.

Renewed spirit transformed mind
Old habits cling desperately to time
Conscience enriched inner peace
Mind body soul divine…
After a change of mind
The body lags behind.

Memories are not easily erased
As time is needed to hide the trace of sins
Raped repeatedly in a subconscious place
Violated
Twisted
Mind body soul divine…
After a change in spirit and mind
The body still lags behind.

Emotions of the soul filters
Logic and anguish
While battle tested memories linger.
So keep in mind, change takes time
And the body always lags behind.

Opportunity

Strike while the iron is hot
Flame intensely burning
Move toward the heat
Sway to the beat
Quickened by internal yearnings.

Talents long lived lie dormant for years
Chance… brief and well-timed Clings
desperately to fears.

Open the window of opportunity
See through the pane of chance
Raise the shades
Feel the blaze
Of progress and possibilities.

When the time is right skeptics take flight
Let the light of opportunity ignite
And strike while the iron is hot.

Crossroads

Crossroad of *life* Seeking
wisdom and advice Direct
and guide my way.

The upper road solid not wide
Is somewhat limited to forward stride
Crossroad of life should I stay?

Or should I compete again on the
Road once traveled
Follow the path of old.
As a wiser person knows
Streets are not paved with gold
Crossroad of life direct my course.

With insight and clearer vision
Should I take the road less traveled
Where raised slopes and eternal hope
Keeps it smooth and finely graveled?

Hypocrisy and pride is curbed to the side
And replaced with determination.
Order my steps bind my will…
Enhance my motivation.

Procrastination

www.procrastination.com
"I'm going too!"
All day long.

"As soon as I finish this it's next on my list"
www.dither.hummm
Remnants from yesterday
Prolong or postpone
www.defer drag on.

Never put off till tomorrow
What you can do today

Good intentions on hold
Download motivation
From the stall mode.
www.jam overwhelm

Back – search – file – away
Review again another day
www.baseline. Delay

Exposed

You can't hide the plank in eyes
The depth of smiles
Broken lines sealed by time
Grief laughter resistance hard line.

You can't hide dreams unfulfilled
The valor of years
Failure or gain
You can't hide pain.

When curiosity rise
You can't hide
When criticized
You just can't hide.

You can't hide tension felt
When secrets are told
Or internal desires
To sometimes control.

Think nobody knows?
You're exposed!

Chapter 2

New
Thoughts
New Ideas
New light
Chapter Two
Sows
Seeds of Insight

Seeds of Insight

Dreamer

Every great poet dreams
Of thunder rock mountains
Of leaves bearing shades of green Of
rocks tucked, nestled in between
Thirsty trails of passing rains dissolved
By noon day sun.

Poets have visions of sonnets dancing
Rhyming with budding verses,
Only to be awakened by glossy written lines.
Recurring images of Northern winds on open plains
Shifting, drifting snowflakes inland.

Poets snooze, then slowly awaken
Nourished under nature's wings.
Poetry is shaken, shaped, wrapped and reborn.
Every great poet dreams!

Political Pandemonium

The country is in a terrible mess
Reporting around the globe.
Money is tight
Foreclosures are in the spotlight
Employment is now on hold.
Businesses are folding Hospitals
overflowing
The Dow continues to drop.
Eyes are on the President
To mask-up and make it stop!

Bring back times when things
Were grand is the country's sentiment

But too few are willing to fess up
As leaders misrepresent.
The country is in a terrible mess
Though it will eventually rebound.
Wars and conflicts in reality
Are much worse than they sound.
Since the beginning of time,
Man, complex and bright,
Has always found legitimate reason
To engage in political fight.

Bring back times when things
ere grand is the country's sentiment

End the pandemic and restore world order
Around the continent.

Universal Songs

There is a rhythm to the universe
There is a beat a flow a tone.
With a tap tap tap… a rap rap rap, a melody is born.

There is a rhythm to the universe
A rumble a growl a groan
Thunder partners with lightning
To keep the timing going.
With a tap tap tap… a rap rap rap, a melody a tone.

Rain sprinkles drop and pour Into
the Ocean it gushes and flow,
Hail and sleet on the mountain top Rattle drop pop.
Tap tap tap… rap rap rap, a melody is born.

There is a rhythm to the universe
That changes with the wind
Chasing itself like a narcissistic beauty
It blends, blends and bends.
Tap tap tap… rap rap rap, a melody is born.

Fine-tuned and tight
Crusty with might
Stuck in the overflow.
The earth quakes, shudders, splits and roars
Uplifting its mighty core.
With a tap tap tap… a rap rap rap
A melody… A song.

Brothers on the Down-Low

Brothers on the down-low where do you go
In the quiet times of the mind
Reminiscing conquests one night stands
As you cover once again?

Into the darkness unsuspected
Seeking same affection.
Plagued by guilt of raw passion
Yearnings and desires.

Brothers on the down-low where do you go
Unfaithful to the faithful
Natural to the spirit?

Incognito cunning and cagy
Watching for visible signs
Of brothers seeking brothers as lovers
Hiding behind the family line.

Entangled orientation, destination alienation
Lifestyle… deception by design.

Justice

Release the feeling
Held so smug
Crammed in the point of a pen.
Remember humans are more than just cases
That so easily become routine.

Render judgement
With the fairness from which you were trained.
Control the notion to let personal bias surface again.

Regardless of the outcome
Life will go on
But for every unjust decision
Justice will overcome.

Endurance

Only you know what you go through
You know what you can endure Only you.
Only you can work out
Your soul salvation
Only you.

The Hot Stove Theory

Sizzle Sizzle Fry
Burn
Premise…
"Touch and learn!"

Play with fire, you *will get* burned.

Touch it once, feel the pain
Touch it twice, never again
Touch it till it pains no more.

External scars
Bruises Burns
Internal conflict
Never learn!

Teardrops

Silver rain
Scattered showers
Drip drop stop!
Resound sound
Tears sweat down my window
Pane. Smell of rain
Splashed against
Red clay dirt Earth.
Wet dusty soil
Waiting to be soaked.

A burst of clouds
Loud! Opened up the sky
From dust to mud
Tap to flood.
Raindrops from above
Drizzle
Drizzle
Drop
Stop!

Chapter 3

Free Speech Without oppression In Chapter Three Are Seeds of Expression

Seeds of Expression

Conception

Creative mode
Tugs deeply at the core
Skim slowly through the passageway
Of haze… maze
Where the mind is rested *Tested*
Where the imagination and thoughts
Are translated into meaning *Reason*
Give shape to creativity
Turn concept into art.

Ouch!

Rings rings everywhere
Body piercings
Do we dare?

Stick little holes through the skin
Let the mutilation begin.

Eyebrows, nose, private part holes
Pricks right through the tongue
Navel rings of platinum and gold
Lavishly adorned with gems
Jewels precious and rare.

Ornamentation
Mutilation
Body piercings
Do we care?

Expressions of the flesh
Permanently edged in skin
Tribal communication
Stories of kin.

Semantics, drawings symbols and such
Markings and paintings stories tell us.

Hugging the body like a giant canvas
Narratives express insight and personal anguish.

Of war and peace
Private reflections
Often communicate emotional connections.

What's important at the moment
Written as truth
One day becomes a fad of youth.

Hugging the body like a giant canvas
Narratives express attitudes and global anguish.

Expressions of the flesh
Edged, pierced or painted
Carry stories of history untainted.

Body Language

Tattoo designs in hidden places
Peek-A-Boo locations Abstracts –
Tigers – Grim Reapers Butterfly
Faces -- Crawley creepers
Showy patterns, simple and complex
A mix of delicate and bold
Textures and prints
“INTRICATE”
A sight to behold
Arms – legs – backs – necks
Body parts Obsession
Creative language
Of sublime perfection.

Stuck

Get out of that box!

Hey, "I'm no square!"
It's warm and safe and
Comfortable in here.

I have four choices
Two up two down
That's all I need to get
Around.

No one expects much of me
I've learned from life
To just let it be.

Get out of that box!

A Tale of Caution

Don't look to me for the model you seek
I move with an unflattering stride.
In a world where materialism reign
I wear the crown with pride.

Demanding trust and dabbling in greed
Preying on the weak and poor to succeed.
I give the nod of approval
Yet, openly practice deceit
Without conscience
Destined to repeat.

Aggressive behavior
Theatre in the round
Dramatic Electric
Broadway Bound.
"ENTITLEMENT"

Mine all the time
A prerequisite of my birth
Transparent color favor
Shielded from penalty on earth.

So… walk a mile in my shoes
Like a rebel without a cause.
Identity
Take pause
Beware of pitfalls.

Outrage

The arrogance of race
Justice erased
Violations of body and space
Engrained in tradition
Tested embraced
Fear…
Tear stained face.

Taste the yearning
Of vampire fangs infused into the veins
New blood
Chilled in cold blood, *Flow* without love
White thirst – Red BLOOD – **Black** drop.

Stop

Put on your listening ears
STOP
Do not speak Make a choice Hear my voice Understand Focus deep
Ask for wisdom
Process
Use the brain and heart
Listen – Think – Ponder
Asking questions sets you apart
So…
Put on your listening ears.

Chapter 4

The beauty Of Nature
Spotlighted
In Chapter Four
Is sprinkled with Flowers
Sun & More

Seeds of Nature

Sun

Golden yellow rays
Eye opening bursts of light
Glistening gently

Season of change
Smell of Spring
Scents intoxicating
Awakening leaves
Flowers and trees
Floral exhilaration.

Dogwood blossoms
Freshen the air
Offering fragrance just before dawn.
Trees leaning slightly eastward
Opening fresh petals to the sun.

Season of change
Showers in Spring
Excess precipitation
Garden perennials Slowly reveal
Growth determination.

Budding Tulips breaking ground
Raises its colorful head
Fancy pansies spread its wings
To fill flower beds.

Welcome Spring!

Flutter

Gentle butterflies carefree and light
Spread your wings in flight,
Against the breeze toward the sun
Pretty butterflies silently perform.

Toss and turn gracefully dance
Sway in sheer delight,
Smooth twisted somersaults
Reaching higher heights.

Bright orange Monarchs
Feast on Marigolds
Prissy Painted ladies
Glide effortlessly and bold.

Light bright Checkered whites
Dance in Spring for you,
Fancy as can be
Cause butterflies are free.

Birdsongs

Early morning silence
Sound of the rising sun
Warm calm peaceful music listen
To bird songs
Sweet sweet melody
In perfect harmony…

Color me pink
Color me tan
Color me yellow
Sounds rare and mellow…

Listen to bird songs
Serene like morning air
Every beat on key
Whisper flawlessly…

Color me green
Color me blue
Color me brown
Surround sound heaven bound…

Red robins chirp softly
Blue jays answer the call
Sparrows blend with all their kin
Singing one and all…

Color my sound
Color My peace.

Rosebud

Roses are Red Yellow and
Coral Violets are never Blue.
I love the sweet smell of floral flowers
Just like I love you.
Sunshine nourishes the vines
Sweet and delicate petals Lilac laced
Citrus trails Multicolored meadows.
Seasonal bloom Roses are born
Roots, Stems, Petals…Thorns.

Clouds

A gentle motionless breeze
Swayed against the evening
Sunset
Horizon scripted
Color coded language appeared.
Spoken spirits of
Blues and whites
Streaks of silver,
Perfectly blended
Stroked the sky.

Dancers, Knights, Giant Sunflowers
And angels
All claim their places
Still peace contained
Calmness consumed
And marveled the earth,
Space untouched.

A picture perfect backdrop
Displayed a masterpiece in progress
Changing with each interpretation.

Snowflakes

No ordinary snowflakes fell from the sky.

Appearing extra special to the naked eye,
Silky flakes quietly drifted
Seeking terrain
Then softly hugged the earth again.
Creating a pure white blanket
To cover a cold Winters' night
Flurries sparkled like diamond cut crystals
Radiant and bright.

No ordinary snowflakes fell from the sky.

Each mirrored the others eye.
Images danced
And flickered at a glance
Erecting a transformational stance.
As trees and branches took on a new face
Slowly dressing the horizon in beauty and space.

No ordinary snowflakes fell from the sky.

Senses

Your survival skills
Into the forest will live
Hear See Smell Taste and Feel

Chapter 5

Where
Words & thoughts
Come alive
Read about change
In
Chapter Five

Seeds of Change

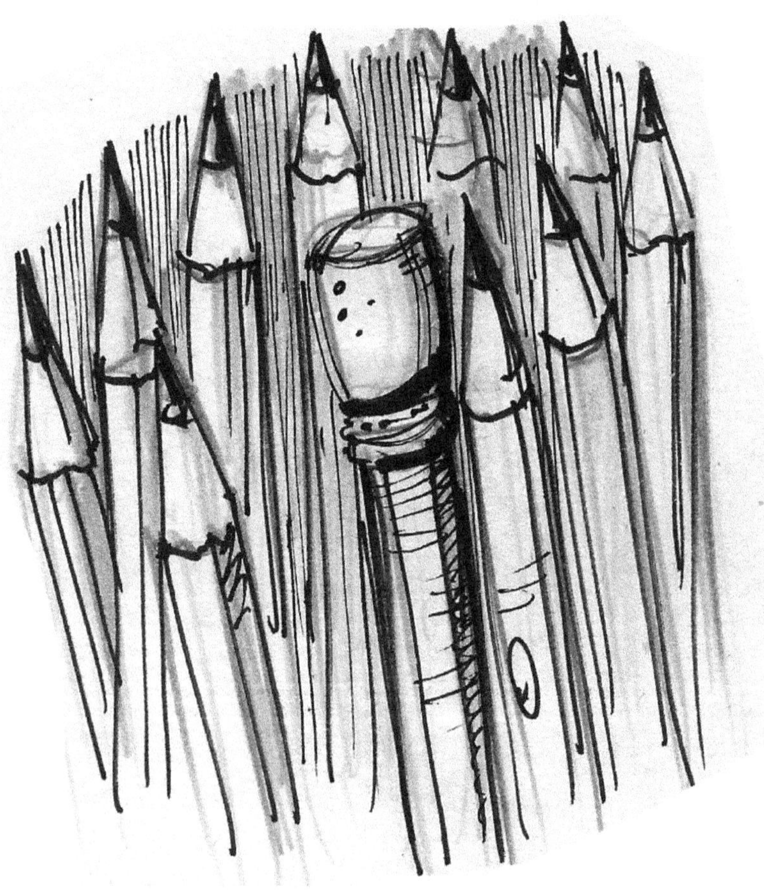

Till Tomorrow

Young Ones wish for
Grown up status but
Clipping wings takes
Precision.
Reality reveals that
Leaving the nest is a
Multifaceted decision.

Impatience lacks insight,
Vision requires more than
Thinking out loud.
Young adult independence
"Carefully planned", makes
Everyone proud.

Flying solo equals freedom
Testing character builds trust.
Transition is a beautiful process,
One that should never be rushed.

Journey

If youth could but reveal the road that lies ahead,
Grace would sharpen the senses and quickly
Redirect forces right before life itself
Becomes that which is focused on most.

If youth could but capture the experience of years,
Wise choices would erase disappointing tears.
Life would smile on regrets and embrace the most
Incredible fears.

Through the process of "live and learn",
Life teaches us that
Mistakes carry costly consequences.
Grown-up burdens heavy laden
Are not just for the young at heart.

If youth could but hold on to time as a reminder,
"I once walked this road,"
Life's path would reveal the true essence of endurance.

Bluebirds

From one little Bluebird to another
Flying together when there are no other.
Chirping and gliding against the wind
On each other they do depend.

"Hey little Bluebird spread your wings"
"Soar above the icy rain"
"Fly real high above the storm"
"Blue skies will guide us home"
"Faith and hope will light our way"
"And we will see a brighter day."

Looking for a place to rest
The two little Bluebirds built a nest.
Eagerly gathering sticks and pests
Both knew they passed the test.

A nest is now built to cover
From one little bluebird to another
They learned to support and trust each other.

Little Sonnet

On life, poets still write
ONCE UPON A TIME

Rainbow light, bright orange, purple and gold
Hovers in the horizon Glowing,
growing shiny and bold…
AN UNFOLDING STORY.

Mother swan gracefully bent in harmony singing
And praying.
A peaceful dove spreads her wings
Uniting friendly relations.

Garden filled memories floral and pine
Seeds creating Oxygenating
Giving back to time.
Yellow and green nourishing roots
Seeking darkness until light blossoms into being.
Water streams offering love fruits to the trees.
Silky vapor clouds time changed
Winding through life
Sometimes saddened by yesterday
Always joyous of tomorrow.

Live life with the heart
And passion of a child
And the wisdom of age.

Gathering

We met and connected unselfishly
Reflected, sharing ideas and views.
As to the direction there was no guessing
No one had a clue.
Was this an open-ended agenda
A meeting of the minds,
Or a one-time rendezvous
Stamped and sealed 8-22-09
Departing there was the feeling that
We would meet again
However, no one knew exactly where or when.
Now, normally this would stand to end
A somewhat perfect day
But fate would make another connection
That could happen no other way.

From New York to Chicago
Two childhood friends reconnected
With forty years of precious memories
Condensed and reflective.
The conversation was easy, full of laughter no strain,
Which cradles the hope that this connection
Will also remain.
Miles nor years did not change the core of our being
So I name this very special day,
"Generosity unforeseen."
There is an unusual link between
The gathering and my childhood friend
Secretly, I'm hoping neither will ever end.

Sun-ash

I write my own story
Chart my own lines
Start a new chapter
One day at a time.

I develop new characters
Independent and bright
Reshape and mold
Every aspect of life.

I direct and cast a brand
New approach
Adding meaning to life
Of which one can boast.

Then edit and give credit
To staff for support
Acknowledge that without them
This story would be untold.

So I continue to write
Cast and direct
A never ending story
Of life at its BEST.

Each step taken
Brought me to this place
Where life is an open book
And the world is a stage.

Teano

Paths cross in all seasons
Brief encounters happen for
Unknown reasons.

You are wise beyond your years
Deeper than
Your childlike demeanor would suggest.

Healed scabs cover open wounds
Revealing unsettled spirits.

I hold you in my heart
To cherish forever,
Warrior Sunshine Friend.

Becoming

I like your smile
Style-charm-grace
Your taste and silly ways.

I like your drive
The pace that keeps you moving on
Your dedication to getting the job done.

I like your conviction
Those moralistic ways
Values and judgement uncommon today.

I like the perseverance you exude
To achieve success
The effort you exert to fulfill your quest.

I like your vision, loyalty and faith
That spiritual connection seeking perfection.

I like hearing you say…
"I do things my way!"

Chapter 6

Bedazzled By Enlightenment & Wit with rationale thinking In Chapter Six

Seeds of Enlightenment

Rehearsal

Agitation started
In the rhythm section
With a slight beat
Of the drum,
Then continued
Throughout the chorus
In every single song.

Fear

I gave fear a body
I gave fear a face
Fear took on movement
Then filled my space.
I began to doubt
Apprehension set in
As fear and I became
The best of friends.

Battle Cry

For every battle fought I fight two
Fighting for respect then I fight you.
I struggle keeping the family in tact
To make your absence less of an impact.
Then with dignity and pride I uphold
And protect your name with damage control.

I fight morning sickness, fatigue and pain,
Nitpicking, gossip and raising cain.
I fight the war of injustice until equality reigns
So that gender and race are “isms” with no game plan.

Fighting for a place in this land of my birth
I punch and jab for dignity on earth.
I battle ignorance, deceit, dishonesty and crime,
I tackle arrogance when my self-respect is on the line.
I fight for those with no podium to stand
Become engaged in their challenges and demands.

Then like a slugger, I duck and shuffle
Swing and wobble until my knees buckle
Back and fore, left and right
I dance to the jam session of life.

Walk in my Shoes

Judge if you must
But you cannot define me.

You don't know my thoughts or inclinations
Internal emotions
All mine
Not up for observation
Judge if you must
But define not.

You've never felt my rage
Or experienced my pain
Success or failure
My measure of gain.

You don't know my heart
So ask for clarification
As false perceptions can complicate situations.

Careful with projection
I have protection
Judgement is divine
Definition is mine.

An intense tension
And entertaining anger
Causes tempers to rise

Rage II

Rage saw red and confronted Blue
Conflict ensued persistence grew.
Rage turned yellow, orange and green
Escalating, threatening, almost obscene!

Mixed with malice, things quickly changed
Rage however, could not be contained.
As destiny gloomed out of control
Black-out consumed Blue in a tight choke-hold.
Now as Blue began to see the white light
Rage took on a different fight.

Incarceration became his motivation
To change Blues' critical situation.
At that moment, Rage no longer saw red
Instead he saw Blue who was now near dead.
His drive to revive went into overload
With time to think and gain control.

Today instead of red, Rage hopes to see
The color of freedom and tranquility.

Me & My Thoughts

Just me and my thoughts
Can't separate the two
We're longtime friends… connected.
Lately we're in a state of contradiction
Struggling against
Rejection.

Without really trying
We try each other
A battle of wit and recall.
Now, as clear as day
My thought is "Red"
But from my mouth
I say "Green" I meant "Red"
"Green", I should not have said.
For one split second
My thought and
I Unwillingly departed.

So quickly… I kept the thoughts flowing
Baffled my subject by not exploring,
Careful not to expound
Just how would it sound?
With a slight adjustment
We found common ground,
Just me and my thoughts.

Hope sits patiently
Lodged between want
And despair,
With just a flicker of light
Hope lingers there.

Instinctively, hope looks
Into the eyes of faith
Stimulated by chance
Belief enhanced.

Hope becomes vision
Vision becomes reality
Reality leads to progress
Progress to success.

Liberation

Now seeking the fruit of labor
Bewildered by what's on the table.

A full plate…

Sacrifice-Provision-Intervention
Generating the vibration of good intentions.

Seeking the fruit of labor
Expecting Godly favor
Accepting the perception
As a pillar of strength while
Praying for guidance and confidence.

Now seeking the fruit of labor
Accepting what's on the table.

Promise

Promises are… good if kept
Promises are… honorable if upheld
Promises are… empty if broken

GOD'S PROMISE IS ALWAYS GOOD

Chapter 7

Chapter Seven
Stands apart
With
Seeds of Love
From
The Heart

Seeds of Love

Seasons

Spring Sings
Of heated passion
Summer Sizzles
With love
Winter embraces
The warm Indoors
As fireplaces fan
The flame
Of love

The King & I

He was liking me and I was liking him,
The relationship started as a casual whim.
"Friends to the end"
Our motto sounded like a cliché
It was an affirmation of noncommittal
What else can I say?
He was my pal, my rock… my king.
Yes! people, he was my everything!
"Inseparable," they called us as we served our reign
Now… there goes that bond thing again!
We profiled, fronted and adored our subjects,
Engaged, uplifted and supported each other.
Then somewhere lodged between casual & just friends
A newly found relationship began.
Ooh! we resisted…Openly twisted our words
Beginning to feel what others already observed.
"Gullible," they called us… In total denial
This monarchy was genuinely certifiable.
Mentally aligned through thick and thin
Somehow cupid was destined to win.
"It was your fate," some said after years united,
One love connection started a whole new dynasty.
What began as "friends to the end," till this day rings true
Friendship before love is
The balance, The test… The glue.

New Love

He walked into my life
As confident as can be
Could this guy be my future my destiny?
Communication
Association
Unlike any you see
Connected and sealed tight him and me.
A relationship that transcended mere
Physical attraction
Neither could control our ultimate reaction.
Reaching new heights
We both termed endear,
The question was…
Where do we go from here?
Slowly parting, it appeared quite clear
That feelings do not easily disappear.
As time becomes a measure of change
Remnants of love still remain.

Proposal

You are my life
My love
My forever man
Right now I want to hold your hand.

Give me the glitter I'll take the gold
The borrowed
The new
The blue and The old.
Bring on the band I'll take the first dance
I want it all…
The vows, The ring your everything.

I want a home, three kids and pets,
Four show dogs and maybe a cat.
I want motherhood, a degree and career,
To juggle it all I need you my dear.

So take my hand forever man
I'll give you the vows the ring my everything!

Compatibility

Start with open & honest communication
Seek
Social Emotional and Spiritual
Balance.
Embrace fidelity & Up-hold morality.
Adore, cherish and remain committed
In the best and worst of times.

Become friends unconditionally
Reframe from judgement.
Listen as well as speak.

During periods of conflict
Work toward resolutions.
Hugs and kisses matter
Try them often.

Recipe for Love

Ingredients:
Communication
Morality
Fidelity
Trust
Affection
Commitment
Patience

Start with a committed relationship
Add a double dose of open and honest communication
Talk through issues until resolved
Reframe from judgement
Love unconditionally.

Slowly stir into the mix
A generous portion of hugs and kisses
Increase the amount until the desired taste is reached.

Add trust and devotion
One ingredient at a time
Blend together until the relationship
Is smooth and balanced.

Reduce lumps
With a pinch of affection and lots of patience.
Take a moral oath to cherish and love forever.

Survival of the Heart

Two lovers separate
Out of sight out of mind
The heart still feels the plight of years
As the soul searches to find.

One love unforgotten
Haunts the mind
One love unforgotten
At this place in time.

A memory born out of love torn
Vanishes…
As the heart flirts with a ray of hope,
Beating to a different drum
Rhythm influenced
Hummm…

One love unforgotten
Haunts the mind
One love unforgotten
At this place in time.

Love searches for a stroke of passion
The sensation of a touch.
Fragrant as a honeysuckle vine
In the alleyway of time.

An unforgettable love.

These Foolish Things

A shadow…
Slowly disappearing from sight
A warm memory
In the middle of the night
An uncanny gesture…
A stranger's smile…
That wanton look in the eye of a child.

These foolish things

A feeling that sometimes triggers regret
An empire dress… A wide brimmed hat.
The smell of earth after a sprinkle of rain
That overwhelming fear of a hurricane.

These foolish things

Appearances revealing two gentle souls
Too young to know what life holds
A touch… a feel… a warm embrace…
A bruised heart
A silent trace.

These foolish things remind me of you!

Shadow of Love

Every now and then…

When the moon glooms
Half masked in the clouds,
When lightning strikes
And thunder rumbles loud.

When the sunset hovers
Brightly on the horizon
Waiting for darkness to fill,
When the air is cool
And the night is still.

When the ocean pushes seashells
Gently to the shore,
Time releases memories
As tides open the door.

Every now and then…

The Happy Heart

Use it or lose it…
What happens to a heavy heart?
Refusal to share causes a snare
Magnified when apart.
Use it or lose it …
Protect the heart from pain
When the heart is happy
It will open
And love will come again.

Chapter 8

In Chapter Eight
Children are
The seeds that matter
Our Hope for the future
Sprinkle
Grow
Scatter

Seeds of Hope
(Children's Corner)

Vision

On the road To
SUCCESS
Always keep
Your self-respect

Honesty

Study hard
Never cheat
Honesty is a quality
You want to repeat.
Try it over and over
Again
Until your quality & character blend.

Shine

You are not an understudy
You're a **STAR!!**
The sun will shine
Wherever you are
Be the main character
Take center stage
Lights—Camera—Action—Engage.
Shine like a diamond
Wherever you are
You are not an understudy
You're a… **STAR!!**

Leader

You are the head
Not the tail
Front and center on the power trail
You are the beginning
Of an untold story
Co-author…
To God be the glory
Destined to lead
Born to win
Next in line of a new generation
A phenomenal sensation!

Peek-a-Boo

When the sun is sluggish
Or just having a dim day
I call on Mina-Rai
To brighten my way.

She chats and toddles
Moves with a slight sway,
Demands and pleads
Until she gets her way.

"Where is my Mina-Rai?"
Fondly I'd say
As she hides in plain sight,
Shouting… "Find me!" "Find me!"
With her eyes covered extra tight
"There she is!"
In merriment, I discover her whereabouts.

Then she flops and giggles,
And crashes with exhaustion
Till nap time takes her out.

My day continues
With a plastered grin
Totally mesmerized from within.

Night Life

I put up a good fight
To stay up late at night
Playing games with time.
Excuses excuses
Consume my energy
To stay up way past nine.

Then morning becomes
Last minute too soon
As there is so much to do;
Wash my face, brush my teeth
Put on and tie my shoes.

Oftentimes I'm overwhelmed
To perform in a timely manner.
For sure my mother will yell,
As my emotions swell.
"Get dressed little girl EXPEDITIOUSLY"!!
Actually I become watery eyed.
Sometimes I sob and whine.
But in my heart I know the fault is all mine.
Mostly
I manage to meet my deadline
With a little help from my Gran.
So I show my love
With a great big hug
As she helps to execute my plan.

Bus Manners

Be obedient on the school bus
Sit quietly… Stay in your seat
No confusion or fuss
Think before you speak
Obey the driver and bus monitor
It is your safety they seek
Drivers must always pay attention to the road
While the assistant helps toward that goal

Good behavior is always a must
As a passenger on the school bus.

I Promise

I promise to be good
Just give me one more chance
Please believe me,
This is not a song and dance.

I will do my homework
When I come home from school
I will listen to my teacher
And follow all the rules.

If only I could just get…
One more chance!
I promise… this is not a song and dance.

Sweetness

You are a rare and precious gem
An amazing beautiful find I call you my "sweetness"
Because you are one of a kind.

I love so many things about you
As your heart should already know
My love is unconditional
From your head down to your toe.

You tickle my funny bone
With your personality and wit
Always walk in sweetness & light
Determined never quit.

The world will one day see you as I do
Watching you grow
Finding your way
I pray God will guide your steps
As you go from day to day.

Remington

My baby brother
Is as cute as a button
He loves me as I am.

Every day he greets me
With a smile
Even when I'm upset or tired.

When I say,
"Where is your nose?"
He points it out to me.
Then he touches his ears
With confidence and pride
And when asked,
He identifies his eyes.

My baby brother
Sleeps like an angel
Mom and I sing to him.
He nods his head
To shortening bread
As sleep angels rest right above his head.

Overcast

Rain came into town one day
And took the sun away.
Tiny drops refused to stop
Which kept the light at bay.
Without a fight the sunny rays
Receded from the sky
Playing peek-a-boo
Behind dark clouds
Floating slowly by.

Suddenly the tiny drops
Turned into a light mist
As adversaries, the sun and rain
Refused to co-exist.
Then like magic
Rainclouds gave way to the sun.
Now children in our little town
Can go outside and have fun.

Newcomer

Three years passed
Since you first appeared
Twelve seasons come and gone.
Graciously
You joined this great domain
We so humbly call home.
Your joy
Casted an everlasting impression
With a smile that made us whole.
You wrapped our hearts
In honey dipped affection
Ever so loving and bold.

Focus

STAND TALL
Like a big oak tree
Be STRONG
Stable as can be.
Stay CONFIDENT
Reach for the sky
God is your
BIG oak tree
ALWAYS
Standing by.

Hearing vs Comprehension

Hearing is not always understanding
What did I say?!?!?
Did I ask you to clean your room now
Or sometime during the day?

Is completing your homework an option or a must?
Time management is an art form
You must learn to adjust

And oh by the way…
PLEASE and THANK YOU are manners
Use them…
They will go a long way

Hearing is not always understanding
Now… *what did I say?*

So put on your listening ears
Ask for clarification
Question and verify incoming information.

Hearing is not always understanding.

What?!?!?

Chapter 9

In Chapter Nine You Will Find Creativity Sublime

Seeds of Creativity (Open Mic)

The Imaginary Zone

I

Where waves flow and lights
Glow
Tracks connect and memories
Reflect
Where creativity huddles
Waiting to arise
The imagination is crystalized.

II

Creativity never sleeps
Flashing signals light the circuitry.
Ideas and thoughts flash and glow
Encouraging connections
To live and go
Into the world to claim the name
Of an unknown being
To new found fame.

III

In the zone where thoughts link
Ideas are generated in the think tank.
Creativity, in order to thrive
Seeks a tap to come alive
Whether prolonged ponder or
Instant gratification
At the end of the day
We use the imagination.

A Night with the Blues

The old dancing Blues knew just when to intrude,
Strolling in unannounced he put me in a mood.

The Blues hugged me real tight,
Slow danced all night
And promised to make everything alright.
His moves were smooth as we sank into a groove
With overwhelming sadness that did not improve.

Now… feeling seduced, My inners cried
"Turn me loose!"
As I struggled to survive.
Still a bit sad, but not for long
The transformation was only half done.

So, one last dance
Without a fight
"Bye-Bye Blues!"
What a blissful night.

Looking for the Swagger

She strolled, twisted, strutted her stuff
But wiggle without sway is never enough.

The hips move
But where is the swagger
That sway of confidence
Sassy Classy!
Body movement and demeanor,
Self-esteem patent pending.

An attitude of pride in every glide
Blending boldness and assurance with stride.
There lies the swagger.

Color of Love

Standing tall
Beautiful and bright
You light up my heart
And fill my life
With love
The color of rainbows

Surrogate

Sweet surrogate love
Undaunted by tradition
Skilled and patient indecent anticipation.

Sweet surrogate love
Discussion cannot contain
Desires implied love justified
Lust undefined.

Sweet timeless love
Show your heart explosion
End the tears of restless years
Fragmented by emotions.

Sweet sweet love
Racked with passion
Peaked by reaction of pure primal desire.

Love gently curled and rested time tested
My sweet surrogate love.

Mother for Life

"I'm like a fish out of water without my babies,"
Momma would always say.
She knew from early on motherhood was her destiny.

Momma was as gentle as a lamb
But when it came to her children
She was a mother hen… Fierce !!
Generous affection momma displayed with ease
Her children she loved to please.

To life her approach was melodic,
Humming and singing children center stage.
Daddy encouraged her self-expression
Calling her a little ball of fire.
His influence was coated with admiration and desire.

We were 6, 8, 3 and 10
When Momma's spirit began to change.
The death of Granma saddened her soul.
But like Superman to the rescue
Daddy was there to ignite the flame.
We watched her self-reclaim.

"Motherhood is my destiny!"
Momma continued to say
As things returned to normal…
Redefined.

Gran's Garden

Walk with me through my garden of tranquility
Where vegetables grow robust.
Harvest time will be rewarding that you can trust.
A narrow trail will lead you to a place in the corner
Of my backyard where
growth meets patience
At the crossroad to get an early start.
Raised is a plot of 8x10 where
Collards **boldly** begin.
Quickly transitioning from seeds to leaves
Sweet Collard Greens aim to please.
They dominate space and salute the sun.
Frost makes them tender as they make their
December run.
Side by side…
Beefsteak & Plum tomatoes occupy a close space.
Marigolds snuggle right beneath just in case…
As predator protectors, they discourage pesky worms
Allowing tomatoes to grow
Healthy, Juicy and Firm.
String beans and cucumbers blossom
All over the place
Drawing Bumblebees and Butterflies into their floral maze.
Cucumbers with their gripping vines
Are forever on the run, their productivity to a gardener
Is always so much fun.
Herbs… oh… herbs of mine!!
Once again
It's *lavender time.*

Competing with mint for fragrance in the breeze
Smelling and dwelling underneath the trees.
Rosemary, Basil, Sage and Tyme
Are all neatly potted near the old grapevine.
By comparison,
okra adds a personal touch

With beautiful yellow and purple blooms.
Overnight she turns into a vegetable
Loosing her beauty too soon.
At her foot are Morning glories introduced only as friends.
However, this personal relationship soon comes to an end.
Adding color and taste are peppers:
Cherry, Green, Yellow and Red Crunchy!
Straight to the table from my garden bed.
At some point in time,
Broccoli, Turnips and Cabbage too
Have all visited this place
Only to find that true perfection
Doesn't happen in every case.
Hope you've **enjoyed** your vicarious visit to my place of
Tranquility
Where I find peace and contentment
Tailored just for me!

The Party

Collard greens
Cornbread Sweet candied yams
Lots of treats
Food to eat
Music slammin!!

Congratulate the graduate
So proud… so proud…
She glides about with poise and pride
Greeting each guest with her casual smile
Silently thinking, "Hope they stay a while"

She waves, "Hey Dinky!" "Keesha, meet Mrs. June"
"We'll talk more about my heavenly mother real soon."
"What's up Rashee?"
"The family is showing support"
"Keep clicking Uncle Mulizam"
"Smile – Freeze – Strike a pose."

She collects and reflects
Reminiscing days gone by
Hi Bootsie!!

"Aunt Jo, this party is great!"
Was her sincere reply.
"Everything is perfect as all can see"
"Thank you so much for making this day special for me"

"Just listen to DJ Renee play all my favorite songs"
"Shanus, remember how we loved this one"
"Oh my God what memories it holds!!"
"You were about nine,
So that means I was eight years old."

Sitting quietly in a space where once stood a tree

Was Ada and Shea from Tennessee
They spoke not as she made her rounds
But the utterance of their vibes made an audible sound.

Feelings surfaced with each warm caress
To control her emotions, she did her best.
Four years of struggle
Seeking a career
This day her fight was with a tiny tear!

Chapter 10

Peace
& Harmony
From within
Is captured
& Highlighted
In Chapter Ten

Seeds of Harmony

Solace

When the frailties of life
Become too much to digest

Digress

Redirect energies
And seek divine intervention.
Make the best of hostile situations
Demonstrating courage and resolve.
Eliminate harm
Or the chance for neglect

No Regrets

Embrace and cherish treasured souls

Dear Ones

Pacify the heart and mind with memories
Sparkling jewels of the spirit

Flashback!

Allow the flow of creativity to enter the soul.
When life's frailties are too much to digest…

Find a safe place and reflect.

Renewal

Everyday should be a Birthday of sought
As each new day
Is a chance to create
Something wonderful and different.

New days allow us to clear the mind
Of yesterday's clutter
And replace it with fresh thoughts and ideas
Thereby creating birth
With a special offering to the universe.

Start each day
By renewing the mind
And the rest of the body will follow.

Labor of Love

A life-line
Yours and mine
Nine months rested…

Felt the passion
Before eye connection
Heartbeat-Flutters-Sensation…

Then the pain
I knew I loved you
Even then.

Connected

When you hurt
I hurt too
I hurt when you hurt
That's what I do.

My heart feels heavy
When your heart pains
Heart to heart connection
I hear-by proclaim.

I cry when you cry
I don't know why
Undiluted tears fill my watery eyes.

Inside I grieve when you are sad
Constantly praying
"This too shall pass."

I give thanks too
Cause that's what I do.

I smile when you smile
Feeling joy elated,
Your transfusion of happiness
Is always contagious.

I'm feeling you
Cause… that's what I do.

Joy

God provides happiness
As only God can
He holds the power
Time released to man.
God is strength
Trust him
Gently call his name
God supplies joy
Not man.

Consoler

Joy came in late one night
And consumed my very soul
She fought for her place
To fill a space
Where sadness had no hold.
Tension disappeared teardrops stopped
As joy took control
Without a doubt there was a story to be told.

Was joy's presence centered
Around prayer or self-disclosure
Or should the mind be unconcerned
With feelings of exposure.

At this stage trust the heart
And keep it engaged Accept joy
Learn to live
In her marvelous embrace.

Rock

You're a metabolic booster
At just the right time
A leveling agent
Natural balancer of
Body and mind.

When my day is blue
You restore jubilation.
My joy, always there in every situation.
Calm distilled
Peace everlasting you give.

On Being

SEEK–Not what already is
ENJOY–The sweetness of years, no tart tears
CELEBRATE–The fullness of life
SMILE–Softly at secrets revealed
FROWN–On sinister appeal
EXPECT–Health par-excellence in generous proportions
SEIZE–Each moment as it approaches

Fruition encroaches.

Chapter 11

A Life of planting
Growing & Gathering
It's now
Harvest time In
Chapter Eleven

Seeds of Life

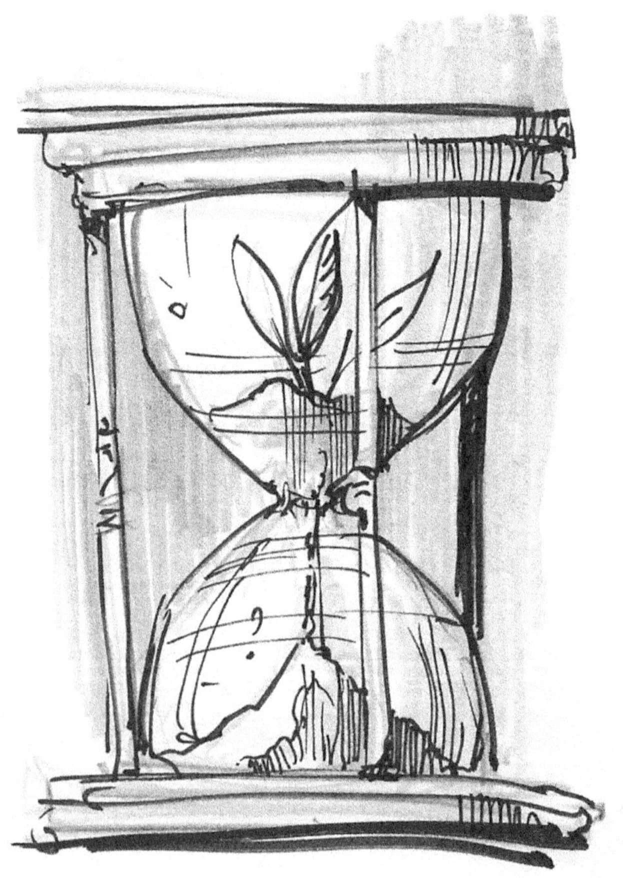

Mammie Pearl

She slipped away midnight clear
Stars twinkled brightly above
Full moon gone too soon
Mammie Pearl my love.
The night grew bright on her exit
Gracing heavenly space
A special tiny angel child
Mammie Pearl wore lace.
They wept as she slept
Embracing life's eternal breath.

The Gift

I was blessed with the gift of longevity
God gave that to me
In addition to time
He safeguarded my mind
And taught me humility.
I learned to love unconditionally
Placed value on family and friends
For in life we get but one chance
And the goal is to please him.

Obedience to the word brings him the ultimate joy.

Release

Each teardrop is like a crystal pellet
Slowly falling into infinity
Cry no more my love
Treasure the times we spent together
Our heart to heart chats
Our spats
Treasure the debates
The disputes and the hugs
Treasure our love.

The East End of Heaven

Dress my room in pearls and lace
Soft white with pink cascade
Fill the air with beautiful music
Harps and strings no bass.

Run a bath of milk and honey
With a touch of lavender scent.
Reserve my room on the East End of Heaven
To purchase not to rent.

Guard my space with Angels
To protect the doors and halls
Hold my abode
On the East End of Heaven
Until my name is called.
Late check in please!

Lil Jo

She lived on her own terms
First child of eight
Survived without blueprint, sample or plate.
They called her "Lil' Jo"

Now, I use to say... "Jo The Great!"
She would say "It's Jo Lillian…"
And when she said it, she said it straight.
There was no twisting or turning to her tongue
"Lil' Jo" was as outspoken as they come.

She walked real fast
Made her presence known
Always had to get something done.
Jo loved to cook and wear her hats
Fast walking… Straight talking…
"Lil' Jo" was the BEST!

On any given day she would let you know
"I am the Big Sista! so what I say goes."
No one could really buck her claim
So we surrendered and played the game.
Her spirit is presently settled…
But, Very much alive
She is now…
Fast walking and straight talking
On the other side.

Peace

I was graced with a love so perfect
He took care of all my needs
But today he came calling
The time has come for me.
I've crossed over to the other side
Reached a higher realm
My savior waits in perfect peace
To accept me as I am.

Relocation

I've moved to another place
Changed my residence
It's tranquil in my new home
No trouble or discontent.
This place is peaceful and safe
A land of milk and honey
No need for material things,
Diamonds furs or money.

Through the Storm

When the dust is all settled
And things are back to normal
What do we do? Where do we go?
Is the pace ever the same again or…
Do we skip a beat naturally?
When the rhythm of life changes
Do memories just fade,
Vanish into that place of forgetfulness or…
Do they live forever in past deeds Positive advice
Silly innuendos in the heart?

When we look to the sky
Is it clear blue or is blue sky altered aqua
Changed by the absence of a smile?
Does the whisper of the wind sing sweet melodies
Then with all its might and glory
Sway trees calm seas
Twirl through the eye of the storm?
Is the Big Dipper, with its high hat tilted
Saluting mightily among the stars or…
Is the dipper just a tiny part of the Constellation
Quietly sprinkling dust over the Universe?
When the dust settles
When the dust is all settled
What is normal?

www.ingramcontent.com/pod-product-compliance
Lightning Source LLC
LaVergne TN
LVHW081301100826
845148LV00005B/936

* 9 7 8 0 5 7 8 8 9 1 4 6 0 *